FABER NEW PO

Annie Katchinska

———

ff

faber and faber

First published in 2010
by Faber and Faber Ltd
Bloomsbury House
74–77 Great Russell Street
London WC1B 3DA

Typeset by Faber & Faber Ltd
Printed in England by T. J. International Ltd, Padstow, Cornwall

ACKNOWLEDGEMENTS

Thanks to the publishers of *City State*, *Magma*, *Mimesis*,
nthposition and *Voice Recognition* in which some of these
poems first appeared. Thanks also to Matthew Hollis for his
editorial guidance; to the writers I have been lucky enough
to be mentored by; and to my family and all my friends
for their support and encouragement.

A CIP record for this book
is available from the British Library

ISBN 978–0–571–25000–4

2 4 6 8 10 9 7 5 3 1

Contents

Bergamot

Not tonight, at least. Not tonight. Now turn your spine
to plainsong, turn the main light off, and shut the door

on the evening's fried buttery food. Time yourself only
to a kettleclick, pour it, stir out the day,

let it darken like a wandering angel. And breathe
in bergamot, the juice of brittle leaves you want

to press against your head, or weave into a dress
in which to rustle on dry lightning nights.

You echo too much, like the fox refusing
to die outside among all the market's

ageing meatcrumbs and fruit. Drink,
burn away your lips. When you cup this hot planet

and hear it turn, you're that rare thing,
a listener. Let moths flood the market

and chew up your city, you're going nowhere tonight.
Not tonight. A scrap of fox whimpers,

cooling its cheeks with old plastic.
Grapes rot softly on string.

Summer in the City

All morning soggy postcards of the Queen's head
have been quietly disappearing from the racks, as dozens
of us have scrawled I MISS YOU IT'S AWFUL on the back
not knowing where to send them. Or so I like to think.
Though perhaps there are others whose knees buckle on buses
crashing through Catford, sometimes, when Crazy Bus Lady, a local
celebrity, throws back her head to howl 'Amazing Grace'
at us, the rattling cattle. There must be others who notice
rain-beaten café tables and secluded spots in parks
where someone is missing, who pass through a square remembering
its Legoland equivalent. By the way, the woman we saw
in her black and white silks and painted misery
is still there, sobbing on the street corner as if all her bones
are breaking to pieces, the hat by her feet glinting toothily
with pound coins. Everywhere I go I hear brass bands.

Crash

OK OK OK *listen*. You mincepied? You roastpotatoed? You goosefatted?
You burping in public? No worries, no worries, come, come and see
what we have here. We have Lycra, pink, green, leopard-print,
and pumping pumping muzak – top 40 type, you'll recognise –
gym membership, yoga mat, swimming costume, Lucozade coupons
et cetera now: listen: carefully: you start and you do not
stop you do not stop look LOOK at her, she did not stop
now look at her bouncy hair and happy children
and the sunlight. No worries, come, come.
If you got the money buy berries, porridge, bulgur wheat,
this exotic polysyllabic lettuce that actually *consumes fat inside you*
or if not, percentages, 3%, 1%, 0%, or traffic light colours.
Sooper-dooper. Nothing you couldn't work out with a piece of paper
and a brain and some time but never mind this is prettier.
This is Comic Sans. This is louder. Come, come.
OK OK OK go. We have our cake. See you next year.

Fairytale

You called. 'I just threw my folder
out the window. Come over.' So I blink against a night
of carousels, of children clutching hymnbooks and pound coins
and crying over gingerbread, your handwriting
of '*this – this –*' skidding along the pink pavement
under a sky snagged in scattered Latin.
Let's live and love, you say, live and love *more*
only look at these toadstools lodged in my chest, look
at my hair, heavy and skimming the ground.
I stand on your street. You want every winter
to be a fairytale, 'But there are mirrors,' I whisper,
'apples, the year will be filled with tricks.'
Turn off your light; feel this air between us; feel it
thick with spinning-wheels.

Too Many Storms

Often, pretending to sleep, I hear my father
in the next room, importantly flicking his books.

Sometimes he hums –
a song from the summer he said he'd hung a thousand wind chimes
in high places, dark places my eyes could never reach –

He hasn't been himself.
He says there are too many storms on this island,
not enough *elsewhere* – and he won't explain,
insists I learn to play chess then snaps
that I hold the king too tightly
and scatters the pawns. I sweep up bewildered ivory.
Now he walks among the trees, kicking all the foliage;
now he's taken to wearing robes of boiling velvet,
whirlpools of blue. He kneels by the shore,
his hands running through bright shells,
half weeping over the clockwork tides,
promising freedom to the air.

I read his books in secret,
thumb the pencil-scratched footnotes
he keeps me awake with. In them,
children have wings, monsters are conquered
by other monsters, men who look like my father
line their wrists with stars and everywhere

there is furious physics,
a sense of time running out,
talk of splintering ships.

Orthodox

Dust bread, dust boy, blood rug, the-eyes-
of-rusty-nails-on-flesh. I make
my church names up instead. I'm eight,
a crumbling flower.

My head is scarved in choir, a crowd
of flame who must have floated down
last night. I call them candle clouds;
they sing for hours.

Shrinking from Adelia's mum
who chatters tall and pink, I'm counting
every saint; old words as strange
as incense ring

and ring to feed me; icons stare;
I stand, a hand to head to chest
to shoulder as Boris drops something,
I hear it clang

between Amens that rise and fall
and fall from girls of melting throat –
from bearded men who sing the bass notes
black, and yet

don't ever breathe. And so I hold
my breath like this is prayer, think as
the lights begin to blur and quiver
I can let

my flesh be incense, pray to melt
or crumble. Assia lights a candle,
burns herself. A wince. That's when
I feel a wax

of clouds and drifting saints and scarves
hold down my tongue – it lets me know
that now I've used too many names
behind their backs.

Toni Braxton

My fate was a weird surname and lipstick that glowed in the dark, and adults who slurred, 'Russia! Russsssia!' at video cameras every year. My parents pinned carpets to the walls and bought a tape recorder, gave me bad asthma attacks with Beverley Craven, Ace of Base, Enya, more Enya. Crawling under the table at dinner parties retrieving furry gherkins and measuring guests' legs with a tape measure, I thought Red Square was full of onions and we'd never go home, and I wanted karaoke not two alphabets, a frog in my throat like Toni Braxton or the woman from M People. The song played simultaneously on Capital and Magic until one day I heard she had to stop begging her heart to be unbroken or her boobs would explode, true story I swore, as somebody's parents filed for divorce and somebody else burst into tears in another room saying they only ever talked to carpets, by now drooping off the walls in a tragic fashion and smelling of gherkins. Say you love me.

The acrobat's daughter

ate cream cakes and wrote the word *beautiful*,
unsteadily, in red pen, said, 'And you have to love yourself,'
as she poured the cheap rosé

we choked on, and only liked kissing
outside the tent while inside a pyramid of clowns
toppled over to delighted applause, and she bit

my ear, said clowns were mosaics, didn't
elaborate. She never did. She let me tie clusters of gems
round her ankles and throat, pointed to bruises, sore spots

where gymnasts with whirling batons, magicians
wielding saws, painted lips and hands
had all tried. She cracked her knuckles and spoke German,

smudged red around her eyes, said red
was the colour of disintegration, only I noticed she said
the same thing when her eyes were turquoise, purple,

jade, orange or blue. She let me watch her
practising somersaults on Sunday afternoons; let me
hold her but whispered that a woman's body was

a natural deformity, someone had written that, she said;
let me buy her sweets she dropped
in long grass, like unwanted flowers. All colours hurt.

February

Tight, tight skin, and the room rings. It matters.

This is February, so she dissolves
smiley faces of vitamin C in oceanic
glasses of water, eyeballs herself and thinks

tendon

tetanus

optic nerve

and someone visits and juggles everything in the fruit bowl
even the grapes, but she binds her face

in white scarves, smears marjoram on her hands. Her
eyes are stethoscopes, her lungs
broken harmonicas, she sees

each minute as a grain of brown rice

laid out on a table, death locked
in scummy bones and staggers
upstairs to Google *-osis, -osis!*
join the dots between

her skin crackling under cotton, rattling
beneath bracelets of eczema, camel-shaped bruises, bitter moths
and the dirt on the window –

the world glows, glows.
Watch her
check her fingertips for flames.

Monk

The chapel flickered like a bloodshot thumb
as I prepared you: tucked loose hair
behind your ears, hung the brown cross
tightly round your neck and kissed you twice –

a ritual. The night was whole for once,
not cut to strips and strands. I tried to hear it
as you scrabbled at the door, pulled me in
by my waist and there we stood. Away

from their vampire grins and tiny witching hours
this, you said, was magic. Here
an eye of orange light, here an altar
like a beautiful cold sheep, and ghosts

and ghosts of hands. I took yours
and we sat, two books of uncommon prayer
chambered in a world that hummed
with glimmering blue-eyed mothers.

Soon they'd weave you to a monk,
dark and primary, and leave me as the witch
who held and needed you but felt your palms
turn dry; who tried to swear

I'd make these bells yours,
catch them by their long tongues
and solemn eyelashes, and spin them into you.
'I'll love you only like a bell,' you said.

Blue

Trojan, I think of you with boulders and innards
and gods criss-crossing your eyes.
I live through days of silence, orange-yellow cheeks
and lentils eaten with a wooden spoon,
remembering the bedroom and the red of your palms
the days you couldn't understand blue,
and waited for a summons – the air you called a shield
would glitter into place
and hard sun collect in your hair, your lashes,
the corners of your mouth. Your blue
is every clink and clash and stab, cold jewellery clamped
to every joint, cold insects sweating in your hands
looking up at the slab
you called bronze, and tried to shine back at
with your blood-smeared sticks of sky. I think
of your body pouring over me the colour of mid-morning;
and now
as you trip
I think of clouds across your chest,
clusters of smiling gods in your eyes as you gape
at what falls as blue rain.

The baker's daughter

is watching me through the reed-slicks,
her eyes surrounded by floury feathers.
Her wings canvas the river. I dip
my twitching toes in her waters, her eyes
pull me in as she says if she could she'd go back,
back to before her life turned owl: she'd give him
all the bread he wanted, she'd bake forever
then pile up his pockets and run, her arms
burnt from the loaves.
My eyes itch like yeast. She says they hate
our flowers and songs, our stupid owlish faces,
and her mud slurps my violets, I sink my knees down
into her fishes and bubbles and claws.
'No girl can ever die honest,' she toots,
tugging me in with her beak.

Kids

This town is full of accidents – his name
that's really a girl's name, the gravel that flakes
off the pavement. They fling it like jagged confetti
breaking him into berry colours.

Underneath an Irn-Bru sunset
we wait, as inside his dad pays for chips.
He tells me lies. That puddle on the ground,
with all the smashed rainbows, that's toxic waste.

Labyrinths

They sweep the hair off the tracks. It's a living –
the tunnels lined with wispy human carpets
connecting Angel to Old Street, Oval to Kennington;
and the walk home, chilly in a dawnbreak
of skin and eyelashes. Learning to see
the world of losses – weekends that finish with
scraped-away lips, street goddesses with grand piano laughs
and not enough toes, nails slammed in doors, teeth
on tabletops.
       And dreams of turning in the serpentine dark,
peering through tangled clouds: holding up brown, red, blonde
handfuls, to cry, 'Look, you left this at Blackfriars, you
who stand there on – what is it now? – Thursday morning, who never
give yourselves to strangers, not in sharp electric light of day.
Can you hear me? Are you OK?'

Temples

Two rhythmic points on a plane of your skull,
twin homes for all the holy ghosts

who cower, muffled, dark dark-eyed
like dormant candles. Let me plunder them.

I'll not be bought off with trinkets and idols
gripped in glass. I'll overcome locks

and protective townsfolk waving their arms,
their mouths like the mouth of the statuette

drooling behind the door; then run
past lilies and bowls of coloured liquid

to the wall, take its timber in my
fists and pull it down   pull it down

for the flaming gods who wait to be snatched and flung,
and loved not prayed at – who pace and pace now

in heavenless black, chew their lips like they shouldn't.
Let me scatter you.

Peach

Juice soaks the sculpted horses' mouths. The men
rising from the foams are catching coins
between their teeth, beneath the morning fruit
that drips the day across each roof and turns
our scalps as pink as ham. Wine on my chin.
My feet pulped into dust. The armless boys
and dogs who sweat in corners, starving girls
who eat their packs of postcards. Waving air.
She said that sun was her sarcophagus,
she told us we should walk and walk. Too poor
for ice cream, sun cream, gulping in the ghosts
of whores and triumphs, turning to the ball
that sings the way exploding fruit will sing.
Just dare. You'll only ever see this once.